Contents

City on the move

Think of London, and you think of two colours: grey and red. There are grey stone buildings, grey pavements, grey clouds and a bouncy, choppy grey river that slaps and gurgles against its stone embankments. There are also brilliant red tulips in the parks, red geraniums in window-boxes and, anywhere near Buckingham Palace, red guardsmen's jackets, trimmed with gold. On street corners all over the city stand dumpy scarlet post-boxes and, in the streets themselves, London's red buses tower above the rest of the traffic.

Londoners queue up patiently as they wait for the bright-red monsters that carry them around. But – perhaps because of their patience – they love a good grumble, and London's buses are a favourite topic. Londoners also know, however, just how important the buses are to London life.

When visitors to London go home again, they take with them a memory of pageantry, palaces, echoing churches, wonderful shops, and lively entertainments. The picture that exiled Londoners keep in the memory is quite different, and is likely to include the sight of a red double-decker bus, coming into view round a corner.

Another memory that a born-and-bred Londoner carries round for life is a map, shaped like a spider's-web made of different coloured threads: dark blue, pale blue, yellow, black, purple, green, grey, brown, and red. It is a map of the underground railway system, usually called the Tube, that can take Londoners in any direction across their city. The colours show the different lines: for example the red line, or Central, goes east and west, while the black one, called the Northern, goes north and south.

The rhythm of London life

These two memories – the map and the red London bus – become part of a Londoner's mental make-up early on, during childhood. Later in life, if London's children become some of Greater London's 3 500 000 workers, many will spend a good deal of their lives in buses, trains, cars, taxis and the Tube.

The reason is that, every day, twice a day, London becomes a city on the move as nearly 2 000 000 people travel to and from work in Inner London. Their journeys can take anything from 15 minutes to an hour or more (not counting those from outside London itself). And this daily rhythm affects almost all aspects of London life.

London today is not quite as big as it was. For many years it was the world's largest city; now it stands only 17th in the international league table, Mexico City being the world record-holder. Between 1971 and

Below: Londoner on the move. The majority of London's people live in the suburbs that ring the city. But huge numbers of them travel into the city centre every day to work. This man will get to know every street on the way from his home to the railway that takes him in and out of London most days of his working life. In the end, he would almost be able to walk it blindfold. London's 'City gents' do not wear bowler hats now as much as they once did. But a tightly-rolled umbrella is still part of the working uniform.

Right: One of London's red double-decker buses finds itself overtaken by pedal power. In the last few years, many London workers have found that a bike offers them a good way of keeping fit and cutting travel expenses at the same time. In traffic jams, a cyclist can often move faster than drivers marooned in their cars.

Left: Almost there. As a commuter train nears its destination, one passenger watches impatiently for the platform to come alongside; others are taking the start of the working day more calmly. Although commuting can be tiring, commuters often say they enjoy the immobility the train journey enforces. Many put it to good use: they read, do newspaper crosswords, even work.

Below: Twice a day, London Bridge is thronged with people going to and from work.

1981 it lost almost a tenth of its population, which is now about 6 776 000.

However, it is still easily the biggest city in Britain and the most important one: the capital of the country, the home of its sovereign, and the seat of its government.

It's in Central London that all the threads of British public life meet: finance, arts, fashion, information, politics. Central London is the place where, more than anywhere else in Britain, important things happen. But they don't happen by themselves. Making them happen is the Londoners' work, and the cause of their twice-daily journeyings.

9

Bridging the Thames

Today, it takes over an hour to travel from one side of London to the other by the fastest method: the Tube. By car in heavy traffic, it would take even longer. But the first Londoners could have strolled across their settlement in something like 20 minutes.

In its earliest days, London was easily contained within the small area that is now the capital's financial centre, the City. Its northern boundary ran in a rough half-moon shape that enclosed two low hills. Its southern one was the River Thames.

It is to the Thames that London owes its existence. (Indeed, London's name may have begun as the Celtic Llyn-Dun, or 'fort by the water': a waterside settlement of Britain's early inhabitants.) When the Romans conquered Britain in the first century AD, they needed a good base that was also a harbour. The Thames gave them both a harbour and a highway westward into the country's interior. But they also needed a highway that ran into the interior of the country from south to north, and so they had to find a way of crossing the river easily. At first they forded it at its shallowest point. But there was a better solution: a fixed bridge.

The ground of the Thames valley was soft and marshy. But, roughly where London Bridge is now, there was a patch of firm gravel on the Thames's northern shore. This was where the Romans built their bridge.

Invasion and growth

Round the bridge's northern end, a settlement grew up that the Romans named Londinium. By 100 AD it had become the capital of Roman Britain, the home of thousands of people.

The Romans left Britain in 410 AD and London's prosperity declined under the Saxons who invaded afterwards. But another invasion brought this decline to a halt. When William of Normandy conquered the English in 1066, he made London his base.

Just downstream from the all-important bridge, he demonstrated his military power by building the castle that would become the Tower of London. But, to strengthen his prestige, William also looked upstream, to one of London's first suburbs. On Christmas Day, 1066, he went to be crowned in the sight of God and his new subjects at the Abbey of Westminster. This, built by King Edward the Confessor and finished the year before, stood on a riverside hillock round the big bend made by the Thames to the west. From now on, London would develop both round its wooden bridge and round the religious centre further up the river.

The two settlements become one

Throughout the Middle Ages (1100–1500), both the bridgehead city and the Westminster settlement went on growing. The lane that joined the two centres, called the 'riverbank' or Strand, was chosen by some of Britain's rich bishops as the right place for building palaces of their own. But the lane itself was narrow, and London's

Below: Roman London as it may have looked about 200 AD, soon after the Romans surrounded their growing city with a wall. Street names like Bishopsgate are reminders of how Londoners got in and out of their city; Bishopsgate was the name later given to the gate in the sunlight on the right of the picture. The building with the big courtyard (or forum) in the centre is London's basilica, one of the biggest in the whole Roman Empire. The Tower of London now stands where the city wall turns to run along the river. St Paul's Cathedral is not far from the spot where the wall turns inland again in the distance.

THAMESIS

Left: All the main sights of medieval London have been included in this picture of the Tower – believed to be the first ever drawn, in 1415. Behind the Tower itself, the new London Bridge stretches across the Thames, with houses and shops on it. Beyond that again is Westminster Abbey, heart of the 'other London' round the bend of the river.

Below: Present-day Londoners relax beside one of the remaining fragments of the old city wall. The Roman Londoners built their wall of stone. The medieval Londoners topped up the Romans' work several times. More than 1000 years divides the age of the wall's footings and that of the brick battlements that still survive in places.

main east-west highway remained what it had been in Roman days: the river, now bridged for the first time in stone.

By the period of Elizabeth I (1558–1603) and Shakespeare, London had become one of the leading political and financial centres of the western world. It now had 200 000 inhabitants and was still growing rapidly. There was a riverside strip of buildings at the southern end of the bridge, and more development northwards, up the Thames tributary of the Fleet. But to the west of the city was still open country and this was where, from the 17th century onwards, Londoners would start building the biggest city in the world.

Below: London around 1600, as Elizabeth I and Shakespeare both knew it. Shakespeare's theatre, the Globe, is the right-hand one of the circular buildings at the foot of the picture. Settlement on this side of the river started early on and, by Shakespeare's period, Southwark had become famous as London's main entertainment centre. Over the river, old St Paul's Cathedral dominates the city skyline.

Change and change again

Fire, war and plague: over the years, London has suffered from all three. At the time, they caused great misery and havoc. But, in the end, they all helped London change and develop to meet the changing demands of the people who lived there.

From the 16th century onwards, London started growing faster and faster. To accommodate its 200 000 inhabitants, it had changed from a walled city into a sprawling conurbation that contained a walled city at its heart. Many of the new districts 'without the wall' were tightly-packed slums that became breeding-grounds for disease, including the dreaded bubonic plague.

For this reason, the noble and wealthy moved further and further out of town to build their grand new residences. They naturally looked westwards, in the direction of the royal centre of Westminster, where the Stuart kings were themselves taking an informed interest in town-planning. James I (1603–1625), for example, dreamed of creating a London that was built of expensive, long-lasting brick rather than the usual wood. During the reign of his son, Charles I (1625–1649), brick was the material used for the new development of Covent Garden: the first London district that was properly planned rather than allowed to grow up higgledy-piggledy.

Plague and fire

The terrible plague year of 1665, in which between 70 000 and 100 000 people died, briefly halted London's population explosion.

But it did nothing to stop the westward drift of the richer, trend-setting Londoners, anxious to find homes away from the unhealthy old city. In fact, it speeded up the westward drift, and so did the destruction caused to the City by the Great Fire of London the following year. But this destruction meant that major redevelopments could now take place there.

It gave architect Christopher Wren the opportunity to build his new St Paul's Cathedral, along with many other City churches. And all the City's new buildings were made of brick or stone.

During the rebuilding, the City's old street plan was kept and this, both through the

Below: 1666, and old St Paul's burns with most of the City. The Great Fire of London began on 5 September as an accident in a baker's shop in Pudding Lane, close to today's Monument. The summer had been hot and dry, and a fierce east wind was blowing; the accidental fire soon got completely out of control. It burned for four days, and destroyed four-fifths of the buildings in London's oldest quarter.

Left: The Railway Age comes to London. The first London railway started in 1837; Paddington Station, painted here by the Victorian artist W. P. Frith, was opened in 1854. Once a railway network was established, Londoners could live further and further out of the city and still be able to get to work. As a result, London started to grow very rapidly.

Below: London in the Blitz. Between September 1940 and May 1941, the nights were made terrifying by the bombing raids of German planes. Central London was particularly hard hit – but, through it all, Wren's St Paul's Cathedral survived unscathed.

street names and the irregular, wriggling street pattern, still shows its medieval origins. Further west, the street patterns are quite different. The favourite street plan of the 17th and 18th centuries, when large parts of the West End were built, was a formal one. Streets were built at right angles to each other, broken here and there by a gently curving terrace or a square with trees and paths. The results of this new town-planning fashion can be seen all over the West End today.

The largest city in the world

New-look London grew to the point when, around 1700, its 700000 inhabitants made it the largest city in the world. Together with that of the outlying suburbs, its population passed the million mark a century later. But this was a modest total compared to the population growth that took place when London entered the Railway Age in the mid-1800s. By the end of the 19th century it was a city of well over 4000000 inhabitants: still the largest in the world and the heart of the British Empire.

Between the Normans' time and the present century, London was spared the worst effects of international war. But this record vanished in the 1940s, when the Blitz and the doodlebugs of World War II tore the city apart. Almost 30000 people died in London during the war, and great areas of Inner London were reduced to rubble. But, as before, destruction cleared the way for new growth, and the tall office blocks of modern London now stand where the bombs once fell.

Below: All change! London's old docklands, wrecked by wartime bombing, are now being reclaimed for other uses. St Katharine's Docks, shown here, provide Londoners with a new marina and the setting for the city's World Trade Centre.

Visitors' London

Londoners are not the best people in the world to ask about the 19 centuries of their city's history. Many have never been inside Westminster Abbey, or climbed the 311 steps of the Monument in Fish Street Hill that commemorates the Great Fire.

Londoners take a comfortably casual attitude to the teeming evidence of London's past, and usually treat it just as the background to their daily lives. St Paul's, for example, is a good place for getting a taxi; London Bridge is just a station, and so is the Monument itself.

But many of London's annual total of 8 000 000 foreign visitors are much better informed. So are the 14 000 000 or so British tourists who every year visit their country's capital. They make a point of inspecting all the main sights of historical London; they read about them first and, when faced with the real thing, view it with eyes (and cameras) that are alert for every detail.

Royal London

To some extent, visitors' London overlaps with royal and official London, with its main centre down beyond the western end of the Strand. Much of London's visible history is bound up with the government of Britain, and many of its most impressive sights and buildings have links with British monarchs, politicians, church leaders, and other top-ranking people.

Top of the visitors' list come the royal homes like Buckingham Palace and the older St James's Palace nearby. Also nearby is the other palace – also royal in its early days – which now houses Britain's Parliament.

In fact, the Houses of Parliament and their clock tower housing the famous Big Ben bell date only from the 19th century. But the building incorporates a reminder of a much more remote past: Westminster Hall, added to William the Conqueror's London residence by his son, William Rufus (1087–1100).

Just across the road, traffic roars past the site of the building where the Conqueror had himself crowned. The present Abbey was the work of King Henry III (1216–1272). All but two of England's monarchs have gone there for their coronations.

Left: A wide gulf exists between Londoners and their visitors – even if the visitors are British too. This young Londoner is not alone in finding something comic about a tourist's bewilderment. But, like all Londoners, she is sure to help with directions if she's asked. Compared to the inhabitants of many other capital cities, people in London have a well-deserved reputation for being polite. Knowing how to behave 'properly' in public – with courtesy and self-restraint – is something the British value highly.

Above: London has few visitors in winter. Those who come may get a glimpse of Buckingham Palace in snow.

Shoppers and theatre-goers

Although London's visitors are usually fascinated by London's long history, other things interest them as well. London is still a paradise for theatre-goers, just as it was in Shakespeare's day. Shakespeare's plays are immensely popular with visitors and, for people who prefer something lighter, there's a big range of musicals and modern plays.

Visitors also enjoy London's museums, its art galleries, and its shops. (Marks & Spencer, in particular, is famous all over the world.) And they love anybody who looks typically 'London': the Beefeaters at the Tower, the market-stall holders, and the punks who pose, and often charge, for photographs.

Do the Londoners like their visitors? On the surface, they pretend not to. Tourists are another good topic for a London moan: "You never hear an English voice these days," is how the complaint runs. But London earns £2990 million a year from its visitors – and, in their hearts, Londoners know that the tourists do a lot of good for their city.

Right: These visitors are planning their evening's entertainment. Much of London's nightlife ends earlier than that of many other capitals, around midnight. But there is plenty of it, often centred on the theatre. London is as famous for its theatres as Britain is for drama in general. William Shakespeare, is commemorated in many of the performances of the Royal Shakespeare Company, at the new Barbican Centre in the City. Elsewhere, over 40 other theatres offer a dazzling range of comedy, straight drama, musicals and thrillers, including Agatha Christie's 'The Mousetrap', which has run for over 30 years.

Left: Trooping the Colour, the magnificent military display that takes place every year on Horse Guards Parade to mark the Queen's 'official' birthday in June. (Her real birthday is in April.) Spectacles of pageantry like this are hugely popular with visitors to London, and with Londoners as well. The favourite is probably the one that takes place most often (and is free) – the Changing of the Guard outside the Queen's London residence, Buckingham Palace.

Living in London

London is full of invisible boundaries. They run down streets, under railway lines and behind houses, dividing off one area of London from the next. Outsiders find them confusing but Londoners, trained by lifelong habit, can trace them without faltering, both in the inner city and further out.

Some of the boundaries are easy to chart: even a first-time visitor to London soon becomes aware of the difference between smart Kensington – home of Prince Charles and Princess Diana – and its less elegant but lively neighbour, Earls Court. But it needs a long-term inhabitant to point to the exact spot where the leafy suburb of Chiswick, in west London, starts turning into semi-industrial Gunnersbury next door.

Rich and poor

Obvious or not, these boundaries and the districts they divide play an important part in giving London its unique quality. Some people compare London to a jigsaw, and others call it a 'city of villages'. As London grew, it engulfed what were once separate and distinct villages (Kensington, Hampstead and, further out, Bromley for example), each with its own history and identity. This helps to explain why each 'village' or district often differs sharply from its neighbours, and is usually seen as a self-contained, distinct community by its residents.

Sometimes, the differences are very sharp indeed. One of the best-known invisible frontiers runs down Regent Street, dividing Mayfair from Soho. Mayfair, one of the richest of all London's villages, contains grand hotels like the Dorchester and Claridge's, several embassies, and many beautiful houses on Park Lane and elsewhere. Soho, famous for its sleazy nightlife, is an area of small urban businesses and tightly-packed homes.

Parts of Mayfair and Soho look very similar. But there is a huge difference between Park Lane's luxury homes, with their sunset views over Hyde Park, and some of those in Soho. It's still possible to find a Soho Londoner living in one room, with a tap on the landing and a lavatory across the yard.

In London, just as anywhere else, it's money that makes the difference. But London is special because the differences between the earnings of different Londoners are enormous. For example, there are more single-parent families in London than anywhere else in Great Britain. (The incomes of single-parent families are often very low.) At the same time, it is the home of more of Britain's top people – earning as much as £100000 a year – than any other place in the country.

Right: Alone, and dominated by a bleak urban landscape: is this how living in London really feels? Like all big cities, London has its unfriendly face, and people used to smaller towns, or to cultures that are more outgoing, could well feel lost and lonely. But even loneliness has its good points: many people feel liberated – even exhilarated – by the impersonal atmosphere of the big city.

As a result of London's village pattern, rich and poor Londoners can often end up living very close to each other. This is especially true in the central area of the city. Inner London contains some of the most expensive homes in the capital, and some of the most crowded and uncomfortable ones.

There are about 2 000 000 people living in Inner London and, rich or poor, there are some things many of them share. One is a fairly short journey to work: five stops, perhaps, on the Tube.

Another thing many Inner Londoners share is the community feeling that London's village system encourages. Neighbours get to know each other, form residents' groups, babysit each other's children, and greet each other in the street. But this community feeling is not so apparent in the parts of Inner London where many people live in tower blocks. This high-rise living does little to encourage a common identity.

When it comes to peace, quiet, and spacious horizons, many Inner Londoners lose out again. Traffic rattles the window panes, next door's music penetrates the walls, and there's nowhere for children to play. A solution exists – but it means moving out. It also means losing some of the friendliness that can exist in the inner city.

Above: The friendliness of the inner city. For these neighbours in one of London's streets of Victorian terraced houses, the street itself is like a shared living-room. Note the tea-cups on the window ledge: the British are famous for their tea drinking!

Right: King's Road, Chelsea, for over 20 years one of the centres of all that's most stylish in London life. As urban pets, reptiles are on the up-and-up.

Suburban London

Although London is so big, and visited by so many people, there are huge areas that the visitor never goes to see. Yet, to some Londoners, each one of these areas is the most important place in the whole city.

This hidden London consists of the thick ring of suburbs that surrounds the densely built-over inner zone: home to about 4 470 000 Londoners, or about two-thirds of the city's whole population. It's also where almost three-quarters of London's workforce lives.

Together, the two parts of the city – inner and outer – are called Greater London, and cover an area of over 960 square kilometres.

London has had suburbs almost since its birth in the time of the Romans. But these early 'outer Londons' – Southwark, Westminster, Holborn and the others – are now part of the inner city, while today's suburbs date from the 19th century or even later.

Right: Posters like this one, advertising rural peace at the end of the railway line, helped London grow more and more quickly as people moved out of town to the new suburbs.

Below: Ruislip village as it really was – and still is. The picturesque church and old houses recall the days before London's suburban sprawl engulfed the quiet country settlement. But, even though houses of the 20th century now cover what used to be open countryside, this is the very edge of London, and the real country isn't far away.

UNDERGROUND

Ruislip Village
and all around lie the
quiet fields and lanes.

BOOK TO RUISLIP.

Cheap Return Tickets
on Sundays.

Left: The heart of the modern suburb is not the church, but the high street. This is the sort of view that, to huge numbers of people, really means London (and home). The railway line that will take workers into Central London is seldom distant. In this case – at Bridge Street, Pinner – it ducks out of sight under the road. The area looks built-up, but a golf-course and several parks are not far away; nor is the little River Pinn.

Below: Dulwich is a good place to live. The suburban children have fresh air, space to play in, and freedom from dangerous traffic. Their parents' gardens, like this park, will be full of rose bushes, and the grounds of their schools will also be green and spacious. But, on the horizon, Inner London beckons and, without the jobs and money it provides, the suburbs would not exist.

Public transport comes to London

Until the 1830s, there were only three ways to get about London, or into it: by horse, by boat or by foot. Horse travel was the quickest, but it was also expensive. Ordinary people could not afford to live further away from their work than they could easily walk.

But, with the coming of trains and omnibuses, the picture changed dramatically. The horse-drawn buses came first, in the late 1820s. The next arrivals were the mainline railways: the first one ran from Central London to Deptford and was opened in 1837. Finally, in 1863, the first stretch of London's underground railway came into use.

Early passengers of the forerunner of the Tube had to put up with the discomfort of open carriages and cinders from the engine in their eyes. But, in spite of these drawbacks, the coming of public transport revolutionized London life. As the transport system grew, London's workers found they could live further and further away from their jobs and still get to them every day.

Linked to the heart of the capital by the new network of bus routes and railway lines, London's suburbs spread out in every direction: northwards to Highgate, south to Streatham, east to Stratford, west to Hammersmith. In the 20th century they spread further still and, today, Greater London measures 54 km from east to west.

Some inner city Londoners joke about their neighbours in the suburbs and the districts they live in. 'Suburban', in the English language, is not a compliment! It implies narrow horizons and a humdrum way of life. But the suburb-dwellers appreciate the advantages of more space and cheaper living. They know that the suburbs can be good places to live in.

But suburban life can have its problems. Distances are big and, without a car, it's hard to get about. It can be difficult getting from one suburb to another, since a lot of public transport is geared to the run into Central London and back. And, isolated behind their garden fences, people sometimes complain they feel cut off. Suburban Londoners prize privacy, but the price they may pay for it is loneliness.

Daily life

Right: With their morning newspapers still crisp in their hands, two of Inner London's two million workers near the end of their daily journey into town.

Left: The quietest time of the day. Under the cherry trees in a London square, a milk float rattles on its rounds in the early morning. Britain is one of the few countries in the world where milk is regularly delivered to the customer's door.

Below: Piccadilly Circus, one of the most famous scenes in London and entrance-point to the city's main nightlife and theatreland area. Most of London's nightlife ends early, but the really dedicated reveller can find places that stay open to two in the morning, or even later.

In many countries, daily life starts early and ends late at night. The Londoner's day, by comparison, starts late and finishes early.

Britain has a temperate climate and, even in summer, the middle of the day is seldom unbearably hot. So there's no need to escape the heat by having a midday rest or siesta. Summer evenings can be warm, but they're not warm enough to encourage outdoor socializing up to midnight and beyond.

In London, the typical working day runs in a straight eight hour stretch from 9 a.m to 5 p.m., with an hour off for lunch.

The human tide

For London's commuters and their families, the pattern of life is so regular that you could tell the time just by watching them. On winter mornings, lights start coming on in

Above: Home from school and hungry. A fry-up with toast and plenty of tomato ketchup is a favourite meal with most British children.

Right: Stocking up. Supermarket trolleys have carriers for the baby but, outside the shop, parents with small children can have a hard time. British culture does not really approve of people that draw attention to themselves in public, and a lively toddler can earn its hard-pressed mum some cool looks.

the houses around 7 a.m., as people get up. Soon the streets in the suburbs begin to fill up with people starting their journey to work.

Before long they're joined by schoolchildren, and by parents taking smaller children to school. Much of the 'school run' is over by 9 a.m., but the commuter flow into Central London continues for a while yet, up to about 9.30 a.m. By 10 a.m. it's shopping time, and the suburban streets are the territory of parents with young children, and of the elderly.

The suburbs remain quiet until mid-afternoon, when the children start returning from school. But, between 12 p.m. and 2 p.m., Inner London hums with activity. For London's workers, the lunch-break is not just a time for eating: it's also when you shop, go to the bank, and meet friends.

Between 2 p.m. and 4 p.m., the city centre becomes quieter. But, from 4.30 p.m., the human tide will start flowing again, back to the suburbs – apart from those who have decided to make the most of London's nightlife by going out to a concert, or a play.

Right: Shopping time, too, for these old ladies. Living in a big city is not always enjoyable for elderly people, who are often worried by the bustle and the constant change.

Right: The London lunch-hour, enjoyed by this crossword fan in a pub. The pint of beer at his elbow is the traditional drink of most of Britain, London included.

Below: It's all systems go in this wet rush-hour. The traffic is being held up by a 'lollipop man', employed by the local council to help children cross the road by their school.

Different beliefs

London has always been a city of church towers. Although they're now dwarfed by modern high-rise blocks, the towers and spires are still there, all proof of Londoners' religious feelings over the centuries.

The churches' names – some of them rather odd – show what form London's traditional religion has taken. St Paul's, St Mary-le-Strand, St Andrew-by-the-Wardrobe, St Dunstan-in-the-West: they were all named after Christian saints. The extra names helped show just which churches were which. There are other London churches called St Mary besides the one in the Strand, and the 'Wardrobe' was where one of the royal officials used to work.

Catholics and Protestants

Although all Christians follow the teachings of Christ, they do it in rather different ways. The London churches that were built in the Middle Ages were the work of Roman Catholic Londoners.

In the 16th century, the beliefs of many British Christians changed. They joined the new Protestant form of Christianity, and this became the official religion of the country. Londoners went on worshipping in their city's churches, but they now worshipped in a Protestant way.

London is a special city for many British Protestants, since it is the home of the Queen. She is the head of the country's biggest Protestant group, the Church of England. Westminster Abbey, where many great State ceremonies are held, is a Church of England church, and so is St Paul's Cathedral. But other Protestant groups, such as the Methodists, also have churches in London, and so do today's Roman Catholics. Westminster Cathedral, with its tall striped bell-tower, is England's most important Roman Catholic church.

Refugees from persecution

Christianity is not the only major religion that is practised by Londoners. Another is Judaism, the religion of the Jews.

Jewish family and public life is linked more closely to religious belief and practice than it is, for example, in the case of most modern Protestant Christians. Worship takes place in a synagogue or 'meeting place', and this can often be simply a room in a Jewish home. There are 185 synagogues in London, apart from those in private houses.

Judaism first came to Britain soon after the Norman Conquest, brought by Jewish refugees from religious persecution in Europe. Many more came from the 18th century onwards and, in London, the East End became their traditional home. A further generation of refugees came with the outbreak of World War II.

Other religions

More recently still, two other religions were brought to London by refugees, not from persecution, but from poverty. Since the 1950s, large numbers of people have emigrated from India and Pakistan to Britain to find better-paid work than they could have got at home. Many of them settled in London, and their children are born-and-bred Londoners. (The western suburb of Southall is an important centre of London's Indian community.) But they continue to practise the religions of their countries of family origin: Hinduism and Islam.

Another group of people who have found work in London came from the West Indies. Most West Indian Londoners are Christians. But some, the Rastafarians, regard the former emperor of Ethiopia, Haile Selassie, as God.

Left: Royal wedding. On the arm of her father, Lady Diana Spencer walks up the aisle at St Paul's Cathedral to be married to the Prince of Wales, according to the rituals of the Church of England.

Right: Islam in London. Some of London's Muslims pray under the trees while the Central London Mosque is built at Regent's Park.

Left: At his Bar Mitzvah ceremony in the synagogue, a 13-year-old Jewish boy formally enters the adult community.

Right: Beautifully dressed and made-up, a Hindu bride sits beside her husband at her wedding. The priest is on the right. Various kinds of food are offered in the ceremony, which can last for several hours.

Left: Sikhs in their *gurdwara*, or temple. Many Sikh families have left the Punjab, one of India's states and the birthplace of Sikhism, to come and live in London, and other parts of Britain.

Shopping

Without its shops, London would be a much less attractive and exciting city. Going to the West End to look at them is a recognized treat for both children and adults, especially just before Christmas. Walking along Oxford Street and Regent Street on a dark December afternoon is a dazzling experience. Overhead, the Christmas street illuminations swing gently in the wind; down below, the shop fronts glow like brilliantly-lit caves; and the air is full of the drifting scent of sweet chestnuts, roasting on kerb-side stalls.

An infinite variety
It's possible to buy almost anything in London, or at least order it. The motto of the famous Harrods is: 'All things, for all people, everywhere'. (Orders accepted and fulfilled here have ranged from a replica of a 1901 Ford bought by an Arab sheik, to a single brown roll, ordered by and delivered to a slimmer in nearby Victoria.) All over the city, goods like food, clothes, drink, books, electronic equipment, cars and jewellery are in constant supply. Variations on these basics may take some finding but, even so, London can offer them all, from books in Japanese to the right gear for rock-climbing.

But London's shops don't just indicate the enormous variety of goods demanded. They also reflect all the different types of shopper that London produces. These include the thousands of office-workers, shopping in their lunch-hours; the Friday night shopping couples, with heaped supermarket trolleys and the car outside; the millions of tourists, loaded down with tartans and jars of Stilton cheese; the late-night shoppers buying some last-minute provisions; and the old age pensioners, intent on making their fixed income go as far as possible.

Tools of the trade
Another group is made up of working people tracking down the tools of their trade, whether these are ruffs for Shakespearian actors or depth scales for designers. London's 'village' system applies to occupations as well as to residents, so the area around Harley Street, where many doctors practise, is well stocked with suppliers of medical goods. Dancers, meanwhile, can find blocked ballet shoes right on their doorstep, in the shops of London's theatreland area round Charing Cross Road and Leicester Square.

All of them will do their shopping within normal office hours, but there's another type of professional shopper whose work depends on shopping in the very early morning. The rest of the time they're dealing with shoppers themselves, selling them perishables like fruit, vegetables or flowers.

Right: Sunday morning shopping in Petticoat Lane Market, in east London. Buying things at a market is one of the oldest forms of shopping and, in spite of London's huge range of shops, markets are still important to Londoners. (Tourists love them too.)

These professional shoppers buy their stock from London's great wholesale markets. Two of the most famous – Billingsgate for fish and Covent Garden for fruit and vegetables – have both now moved away from the sites they occupied for centuries. But Covent Garden is still a lively centre for shoppers, with its cafés, its stalls selling craft goods, and its buskers.

Although the best-known shops in London tend to be very grand or very specialized (or both), the places that Londoners probably love most are neither. From the centre to the suburbs, London is dotted with old-style corner shops. Their owners, who often live over the shop, keep old-style hours – long ones – and sell sweets, newspapers, and a lot else besides.

Above: Jumble – or second-hand – sales are a favourite way of raising funds for local good causes, and there are plenty of bargains for everyone.

Left: Harrods, as glorious by night as it is by day. It's visited by a daily average of 50 000 customers, many of them from overseas.

Above: Whatever you're looking for to buy, you can probably find a shop in London that specializes in just what you require.

Growing up in London

London children, like all Londoners, share the daily experience of travelling to and from work that results from living in a large, sprawling city. The only difference is that their work doesn't bring a wage with it!

Even toddlers learn about travelling before they really know what travelling is. Daytime baby-sitters – such as grannies who live with the family – are rarer in Britain than in many other countries. So, when a well-off suburban mother goes shopping, she loads the baby into the family's second car along with her shopping baskets. An inner-city mother, however, may have a harder job. It's not easy to get a baby, a folded push-chair, and several supermarket bags on to a bus. And, if the lift has broken down at home, it's no fun lugging them all up to the seventh floor.

British children start school when they are five (although some go to nursery school earlier), and it's then that the journeying really begins. As in a country village, school may be only just round the corner. But, especially in the suburbs, it can be round a great many corners, or even a bus-ride away.

Right: However small they are, Londoners are inventive when it comes to things to play with. The old bath could be a boat, or a toboggan; it will do nicely as either.

Below: Inner-city fishing. The waterway shown here is not the Thames, but the Grand Union Canal that runs in a big loop round north London. Although it's an artificial watercourse, the Grand Union can be just as attractive as the Thames to Londoners with time on their hands – and it's just as wet!

London's size can make themselves felt. Just going to see your friends after school can set you on your travels again. Getting to the place where riding, judo or dancing is taught can be time-consuming and difficult, though it's usually worth the effort.

A worse problem is money. Many of London's activities are free, but plenty are not. Although the whole area is the wealthiest in Britain, London children are not among the country's richest. (A survey done in 1985 showed that they come only fifth in Britain's pocket money league.) If their parents are well-off, this might not matter. But many of London's children, especially in the inner city area, come from families who are poor, or who may even be homeless.

If you are poor, London can be a bleak, unfriendly place to grow up in. But it is never boring. If official entertainments cost too much, young Londoners are experts at making unofficial ones. Londoners are resourceful people and this, like the journeying habit, is another thing that they learn young.

Above: Painting a mural on an inner-city wall. Some people have realized that London can be a difficult place to grow up in, and arrange special opportunities like this one for young Londoners to enjoy themselves.

Below: Football practice in the shadow of the gasworks. Although London is full of parks and gardens, they are not always in the right place, and many of them ban ball games anyway. These three enthusiasts have found a practice area where nobody's going to bother them.

Secondary school, to which children transfer when they're 11, is often further off still. And journeys can become as long as those of an adult worker if children go to one of London's independent schools, for which their parents pay fees. Trains, buses and the Tube all carry some of London's schoolchildren to work, and some senior pupils even ask if they can use the teachers' car park. (You're allowed to drive a car when you're 17.) The British school-leaving age is 16, but well over a third of young Londoners choose to stay on for further study.

What about leisure time?
School ends in the mid-afternoon, and weekends are also free. London then becomes full of exciting things to do, from scaling the play equipment in the park to discos, taking in on the way a huge range of museums, sports clubs, cinemas, theatres (some specially for children), zoos, and leisure classes.

But, here again, the problems caused by

London at work

Below: For most London workers, office blocks like this one are the setting in which they spend eight hours a day, five days a week, 48 weeks a year. The buildings look impersonal, but most workers make their own desks and corners into little outposts of home with plants, pictures of their families, and postcards sent back by friends on holiday.

Ever since the Romans made London an important trading centre, the people of Britain have flocked to the city to find work, fame and wealth. Young Richard Whittington, who arrived from Gloucestershire in the late 1300s, found all three, and became Mayor of London four times. (The stories about his cat, however, are just legends.) Then and now, London is the main place in Britain where important people live, where decisions are taken, and where the money is made.

It was as a businessman that Dick Whittington made his fortune, and there are plenty of modern Londoners who intend to follow his example. Their offices are spread out throughout the city but the real business centre is the area of narrow streets and towering office blocks to the east of St Paul's Cathedral. This is the City with a capital 'C', also known as the 'square mile', and it's the oldest part of London.

Buying and selling

Like much else in Britain's capital, the City of London owes its place in the nation's life partly to accident and partly to the river. Where the Thames went, trade followed; and money followed trade, making London the trading centre of the world. Traders wanted to find ships for their cargoes, and insurance for both goods and ships. To buy goods, they needed to borrow money – to be paid back when (and if) they succeeded in selling them. And, to make selling them easier, they needed the help of middlemen who knew the best markets.

It was naturally convenient for the merchants, and for the bankers, insurance brokers and other businessmen who served them, to congregate in the same places. In the late 17th century, they formed the habit of meeting in the fashionable coffee houses that were becoming part of the London scene. One of them, Edward Lloyd's in Tower Street, is today the world-famous international insurance market. Another, Jonathan's, evolved into the Stock Exchange.

Londoners in luck

The thousands of 20th century workers who pour into the City of London every day are among the luckiest in Britain. This is because there is more new work going on in the City, in jobs like banking and insurance, than in any other part of British industry.

But all London workers are lucky in two important ways: not only are there more jobs here than in many other places in Britain but they're better paid too. London women, in particular, do better than anywhere else in the country.

London workers include the country's most famous and most powerful people: its sovereign, its government and Members of

Parliament, and its top civil servants. But they are in a tiny minority when compared to the Londoners who earn their living by making things, either by hand or in factories. And the craftsmen and factory workers are also in a minority when compared to all the Londoners who are in the 'service industries': the work that keeps everyone in the city fed, clean, healthy, entertained – and able to work. Among the service workers are taxi drivers, refuse collectors, doctors, nurses, and caterers. Life in London is so complicated that almost everyone really works for everyone else.

Above: Shirley Williams, one of the founders of Britain's Social Democratic Party, invites the camera to take in her famous surroundings; the lens, however, catches the Clock Tower of the Houses of Parliament at a less than solemn angle. London's workforce includes both political figures and a huge army of government workers.

Above: On the buses. Transport looms large in the lives of most Londoners, so many of them make their livings at it. Almost two-thirds of London's women work – one of the highest proportions in the country.

Left: Work in London is mainly geared to service industries, from government to running a fruit stall. But the service workers all need services themselves. One of them is provided by this street entertainer in Covent Garden: his skills are appreciated both by the shirt-sleeved Londoners on the pub balcony, and by the visitors to London down at pavement level.

London at play

When at home, the British have a reputation for taking their fun rather sadly. This is not true, but they do prefer on the whole to keep their fun a home-based, private, family affair.

A visitor walking through a London suburb on a winter Sunday might think that the whole population had emigrated! Only the blue light from the television, glimpsed through people's net curtains, shows that there's anyone left in the world.

There would certainly be more people around in summer, washing their cars, gardening, doing up the house. But the visitor – an Italian, perhaps, used to a lively street life – would be puzzled at the lack of chat and cheery calls across the road. In the outer city, where two-thirds of all Londoners live, casual sociability is not really the London style. Instead, Londoners keep their chatty side for places and times that are recognized by everyone as carrying the 'social' label.

The pub is a social place (especially when it's the headquarters of a crowd of friends);

the Tube most definitely is not. All clubs and places for shared activities – like allotments, keep-fit classes or even (for parents) the school gate – have sociability built in. You lose half the fun of breeding fancy mice or growing cacti if you can't talk about it with other enthusiasts.

Londoners and sport

Londoners have the pick of the country's plays, films and concerts close by. But these attractions, tempting though they are, often fail to tempt Londoners out of both their shyness and their homes. But there is one thing that, for enthusiasts, will break down even the worst case of London reserve: the city's magnificent range of sports, with football in top place.

Wembley Stadium, in London's western suburbs, holds 100000 people, and is packed out for the Football Association's annual Cup Final. London football teams like Arsenal, Queens Park Rangers, Tottenham Hotspur, West Ham and Chelsea are among the best in Britain, and are a favourite topic with their fans, whenever and wherever these meet.

But football is only one of London's sporting activities. Londoners can also watch cricket at Lord's and the Oval, rugby football at Twickenham, and tennis at Wimbledon, and play them all at hundreds of suburban clubs. (In some suburbs with a rural atmosphere, cricket is still played on what used to be the village green.)

Golf is another sport played in outer London – and, further out still, there's horse racing at Epsom (just in Surrey). Excitement here reaches a peak on Derby Day in June.

Below: This Thames-side path in Chiswick, west London, is the scene for two of London's favourite pastimes. Jogging is increasingly popular with Londoners, and meeting friends in a pub always has been popular. If it's fine enough to go outside, that makes a pleasant occasion even pleasanter. Chiswick Bridge, just visible in the background, is where the annual Boat Race ends.

Left: The British are a nation of gardeners, and the peak of the British gardener's year is the Chelsea Flower Show, held in London every May. After the show is over, visitors can buy the exhibits: a chance to own some of the most beautiful plants in Britain.

Derby Day is traditionally one of the greatest of Londoners' days out.

Another special day for London sport takes place earlier in the year, when crowds of Londoners, well wrapped up against the spring wind and rain, throng to the edge of the Thames to watch Oxford and Cambridge row their annual Boat Race from Putney to Mortlake.

The number of people attending football matches is dropping, and many more Londoners watch sport on television than follow it in person. But, if there's a dog in the house, the most stay-at-home Londoner has to get a daily dose of fresh air. The British are fond of pets and Londoners are no exception; dogs are often to be seen, walking decorously beside their owners, in even the most built-up areas. In the parks and open spaces, they rush around, play, retrieve, fight and bark all they want to – and, like all pets, help introduce their owners to each other. For Londoners, dog-owning is a club like all the rest and one of the biggest.

Right: Like the rest of the British, many Londoners love animals. But it's difficult to keep a pet in a top-floor flat, let alone a pet pig. The children's section of London Zoo in Regent's Park helps make up for the lack of opportunity to do so.

Above: Trafalgar Square – and a young Scottish football fan finds time to explore some of the main attractions on London's tourist beat. But what really interests him is the big match later on.

31

Celebrations

When they find themselves in a crowd in the street, Londoners, as usual, tend to be quiet and self-contained. But there are occasions when they forget all the unwritten laws that make their public behaviour so restrained. When the moment is right, they shout, cheer, laugh, jostle, dance, climb lamp-posts, and generally go in for something called 'mafficking'.

To maffick is an activity that dates back to the Victorian period and the Boer War in South Africa. When the siege of the British garrison at Mafeking (now Mafikeng) was relieved in 1900, Londoners took to the streets in joy – and a new word was invented to describe their riotous celebrations.

Letting off steam in public

Perhaps the greatest example of mafficking were the celebrations at the end of World War II (1945). But the Silver Jubilee in 1977 and the royal weddings in 1981 and 1986 gave Londoners the opportunity to let rip on a citywide scale. And even an ordinary year brings reminders of what Londoners can do when they feel it's all right to let off steam in public.

One of them takes place on New Year's Eve, when Trafalgar Square is packed with shouting, singing merry-makers, determined to see in the New Year in proper style.

Left: It gets dark very early on December afternoons, but Londoners make full use of their dark winters. Without the gloom, the Christmas decorations in Regent Street would lose much of their sparkle.

Below: High summer, and Londoners take to the streets for the annual Notting Hill Carnival. Carnivals like this were brought to London from across the Atlantic, by Londoners whose family origins are in the West Indies. They take place in some other districts where West Indian Londoners have also settled.

Left: Easter brings a couple of days' holiday to Britain. London celebrates it with special parades like this Easter Sunday one in Battersea Park, south of the river.

Below: Not all Londoners use the same calendar for their festivals. The Chinese New Year, here celebrated with the traditional Dragon Dance, is in late winter.

For the really bold, the traditional thing to do was to plunge into the fountains for a midnight dip. But this is much frowned-on by the authorities!

The same sort of enthusiasm erupts on any occasion involving the royal family, though it's shown much more respectfully. Many of London's regular festivals and celebrations are organized round the figure of the British monarch; they are especially popular with London's visitors, but Londoners love them too. The most popular is the parade called Trooping the Colour (or regimental standard), which is held every year on the Queen's official birthday in June (there is a picture of this on page 15).

Another great London procession features not the Queen, but London's most important commoner: Dick Whittington's latest successor, the annually-elected Lord Mayor. This procession, in which the Lord Mayor of London rides through the City in his magnificent gilded coach, dates back to an even earlier time than Dick Whittington's. Its intention was to show the new Lord Mayor to the people of London after his election earlier in the year. But it was only in the 19th century that the procession started to take its present route; earlier, the Lord Mayor took the oldest route in London, and travelled up the Thames in a ceremonial barge.

Winter festivals

The Lord Mayor's procession is held in November, and several of London's main festivals are in fact winter ones. They often involve lights. Christmas, for example, brings not only the West End decorations but also carol-singing round the illuminated Christmas tree (an annual present from the people of Oslo) that towers high over Trafalgar Square's fountains.

There's also Bonfire Night: 5 November, the anniversary of the day Guy Fawkes was discovered in his attempt to blow up the Houses of Parliament in 1605. It's celebrated with much enthusiasm all over London with bonfire parties and firework displays. Beforehand, children display home-made dummies of Guy Fawkes in the streets and ask passers-by for a 'penny for the guy'.

Some London children also celebrate another autumn festival: Hallowe'en. They disguise themselves and roam round playing the American game of 'trick or treat'. Although this is a new custom for Londoners, its beginnings go back many centuries to the days when people believed that the end of October was a time of ghosts, witchcraft and trickery.

London's weather

London is always thought of as the fog capital of the world. Part of this reputation is certainly based on fact, but it has been enormously strengthened by the image of historical London that's put across by film and television. In this other London, where fact and fiction merge, Sherlock Holmes and Dr Watson swirl through the mist in their hansom cab, while Jack the Ripper prowls through the murky streets.

The city's infamous smogs – smoke-laden fogs – have been more deadly than the Ripper in their effects: 4000 people died in the smog of 1952, and another 750 died in another one ten years afterwards. But this smog of 1962 was the last of the real killers to be recorded. In 1956, clean air laws had been introduced and, as a result, the traditional 'pea-souper' of old London is now a thing of the past.

Weather tricks

However, London continues to be a river city. Rivers and mist go together, and misty days are still a normal occurrence. So are wet ones. So are dry ones, hot ones, cold ones. Temperatures in London, as in any big city, are kept two degrees above normal by the heat which leaks from buildings. But London shares with the rest of Britain a pattern of tricky, changeable weather. Surprises are commonplace and, in a climate that can produce snow in May (a summer month), it's no wonder that the weather is often the subject the British choose for opening a conversation.

Hot, cold and coldest

In the summer of 1976, for instance, the city sweltered as temperatures soared to 35°C. In February, 1947, they stayed at a below-zero average for a whole month. February 1986 was almost as cold. In February 1965, however, there was a heatwave: office workers shed jumpers and jackets and sat outdoors in the squares to eat their lunches and to sunbathe.

Earlier records show more extreme weather still. In 1891, a train leaving London's Paddington Station for Devon got caught in a blizzard; it stayed stuck in a

Above: The sun comes out in St James's Park, and brings out London's sun worshippers.

Right: Rain stops play. The summer of 1985 was one of the wettest and most miserable that Londoners can remember. Here, crowds at Wimbledon sit patiently under their umbrellas as the courts are protected against the downpour.

suburban snowdrift for four days. In 1740, London even had a full scale hurricane that damaged the spires of Westminster Abbey.

Most famous of all, there was the winter of 1683–4, when the Thames froze over for six weeks and a great Frost Fair was held on it. The diarist John Evelyn described the frozen river being used as a highway by coaches; other events included "sliding with skates, a bull-baiting, horse and coach races, puppet plays." The ice proved so strong that it could support a fire big enough and hot enough to roast an ox whole.

More sunshine for Londoners

In fact, there have been several frost fairs on the Thames, the last one being held in the early 19th century. Although people have skated on the river since, the weather has never returned to the 'little Ice Age' conditions of the 17th and 18th centuries. Today, the average London temperature does not drop much below 4°C in winter.

London's summer peak temperature is about 18°C. The city is in the drier, sunnier half of Britain, and the decrease in pollution allows today's Londoners to enjoy half as much more sunshine again as their parents did. And enjoy it they do: on blowy March days, when the crocuses are out in the parks; on bright October ones, when there's a crispness in the air; and above all on fine days in high summer. The buildings throw a cool shade, and the light between them is as brilliant as a diamond.

Above: Thanks to the influence of the nearby Atlantic, Britain has a climate that is milder than many countries on the same latitude. Rain is common; snow less common. But many Londoners delight in the occasional snowfall that does take place, and rush out with their toboggans to the nearest slope, in this case in Hampstead.

Right: During this 1948 fog, policemen were needed just to take people across the road. Traffic came to a halt, shipping was suspended, and aircraft were grounded. But, bad though this fog was, it was not as catastrophic in its effects as the smog of 1952.

Outdoor London

More than any other capital city in the world, London is close to nature. Around its outer limits stretches the Green Belt, an area of rural land protected against the encroachments of housing development. Even in the centre it's possible to see green grass, trees and flowers. A lot of this greenery arrives by accident. The old walls of London's railway stations, for example, are bushy with sweet-smelling purple buddleia, whose seeds have been planted there by the wind, and on a Brixton building site, bee orchids have been found growing.

Londoners themselves, however, have been responsible for planting the little apple trees that have sprung up here and there in odd corners: they started as the pips in someone's lunchtime apple.

Alongside all the unofficial gardens, there are thousands of official ones, carefully planned and beautifully tended by their owners. These range from royalty and local councils to all the people who own the traditional 'cat's-scratch' of Inner London: the tiny front garden and a narrow strip of land at the back.

In summer London's rail commuters, travelling behind the backs of houses, are treated to a day-by-day display of what Londoners can achieve with their little patches of land. With their roses, vegetables, lilac trees, ponds and even – though it's a tight fit – swimming pools, no two gardens are ever the same.

Below: For some Londoners, an outdoor life is a round-the-clock reality rather than a way of describing hobbies or leisure pursuits. London sees great extremes of wealth and poverty: this old lady has made a temporary home for herself at a bus-stop in Mayfair, the richest of London's 'villages'.

Enjoyment for kings and commoners

It's every Londoner's dream to have an outdoor space to call their own. But those who don't have one can still get their fill of fresh air. London's parks are gardens for everyone.

Several of them originated as royal hunting grounds, in the days when the West End was still open country. It was Charles I who first allowed the public into Hyde Park. His son, Charles II, did the same for St James's Park. Richmond Park, in the south-west suburbs, is another ancient hunting ground of British kings, and still has deer living in it.

In spite of London's tricky weather, Londoners make full use of their open spaces. During the lunch-hour on a fine day, the parks and squares of Inner London are crowded with office workers, eating, chatting, sunbathing, listening to their

personal stereos, feeding the birds, or simply lying on the grass and staring at the sky.

If they work in the right area, they can have water too. Anywhere along the banks of the Thames is a favourite spot for lunching and strolling. So are the banks of London's other inner-city waterway, the Grand Union Canal. This canal flows in a big curve round the north of London, from the Docklands to Brentford, becomes the Regent's Canal in the neighbourhood of Regent's Park, and is a popular centre for boat trips in traditional canal barges. Most of them start in one of London's most attractive 'villages': the well-named Little Venice, just north of Paddington Station.

Further north still, four miles from London's centre, is the open space that Londoners probably love best of all: Hampstead Heath. This is also a park, but a wild one, and it is here that Londoners can really feel in the country. They can also sail model boats, swim, fly kites and – in August – visit the famous Bank Holiday fair.

Above: Every scrap of earth counts in this London garden, densely planted with flowers and shrubs. In summer, Londoners often treat their gardens as an extra room. They become the preferred setting for eating, entertaining and just living – as long as it doesn't rain!

Left: Wide open spaces. On Hampstead Heath, which overlooks Inner London from the north, there is plenty of room to walk, run, play – and bark.

Wild London

Not all Londoners are human! London offers non-humans safety from hunters' guns in the countryside, rich supplies of food, and a wide variety of habitats – from rubbish dumps to tower blocks. So it forms an ideal, if slightly unorthodox, home for a huge number of non-human species.

There are plenty of mammals, of which the biggest are Richmond Park's deer. There are amphibians, like frogs and toads, and a large number of fish; the clean-up of London's air has been accompanied by a clean-up of London's river, and almost a hundred fish species have been recorded there. There are a great many birds, and countless swarms of insects.

Some of these other Londoners are domestic animals: dogs, cats, carp in ponds, and even bees. But the vast majority are wild. They organize their own lives and regulate their own breeding. Some species are regularly fed by humans, but their lives don't depend on these hand-outs; it's just that hand-outs make survival easier.

Many creatures, of course, are more likely to get a dose of pesticide from human Londoners than a free lunch. But wild London can usually do without the goodwill of London's people, as long as these continue to leave food wastes around and build structures that can be adapted as homes.

Bird commuters

Often, not much adaptation is needed. In nature, the rock doves from which London's pigeons are descended nest on cliff ledges. One ledge is much like another, and the curly stonework on London's Victorian buildings offers a perfect nesting site to the celebrated birds of Trafalgar Square. Kestrels – also cliff-dwellers in the wild – are another species that likes living on London's high-rise buildings; they are especially fond of the modern towers of the Barbican in the City.

Although the pigeon is certainly London's most famous bird, the starling runs it close. At dusk, the whole area round Piccadilly and Trafalgar Square echoes with a noise like rushing water. It's the chatter made by the city's enormous flocks of starlings as they settle down for the night.

Right: Who needs who the most? Visitors to London delight in the pigeons that settle all over them; for the pigeons themselves, the visitors are a cafeteria that never closes.

Below: Starlings at dusk in Central London. From time to time, a flock takes to the air and makes a chattering, rustling flight round their roosting spot before settling down again for the night.

Like the humans streaming towards the Tube stations far below, London's starlings are commuters. They spend the day hunting for food in suburban gardens. Returning to town, they pass London's flocks of seagulls on the way out. These prefer to spend quieter nights in the suburbs' reservoirs.

Down at ground level

On the ground, London's wildlife is less obvious, since much of it is nocturnal. But, like the birds, it's quite often easy to hear, especially in the quiet of a suburban garden. Was that really a dog yelping in the night? Foxes yelp, too.

Hedgehogs make no secret of their presence, either. They snuffle, grunt and (when hibernating in a pile of leaves) snore. Many suburban Londoners put out milk each night for hedgehog visitors, and can tell when a hedgehog's there just by listening. The plants in the flowerbeds suddenly start to rustle, and there's a puttering noise like a moped, heard a long way off. That's the sound of a hedgehog on the prowl!

Above: Old-style metal dustbins have heavy lids that fit quite tightly. But this is no deterrent to a hungry fox, foraging in the night round suburban back doorsteps.

Right: Hedgehogs are friends to London gardeners, since they eat slugs and other pests. But other forms of meat exist too, and the plastic bin-liner is no obstacle at all.

London River

There are many ways of summing London up: Britain's capital, world business centre, a city steeped in tradition, and so on. But the oldest description is also the most important. The name, if the theories are right, says it all: Llyn Dun, the fort by the water.

From its earliest hazy beginnings, London has above all been a place by a river. Without the river to provide livelihood and protection, the first dwellers in the London area would not have settled there. When the Romans came, it was the river and the bridge they built over it that started the city off on its recorded history.

All through the medieval period and up to the time of Shakespeare, the Thames remained the vital bringer of traffic and trade. Although London spread out away from its early riverside site in the centuries that followed, its prosperity stayed tightly linked to commerce and this – for an island nation – was in turn naturally linked to water transport.

Memories of an imperial past

London River, as people often called it, brought shipping, cargoes, business and business services like insurance and banking to the British capital and, by the 19th century, London dominated world trade.

To handle the huge amounts of river traffic now involved, docks were built to the east of the City and their names – the Royal Victoria, the Royal Albert, the West India – carry strong memories of Britain's imperial past and its economic power.

Today, Britain – and London with it – occupies a much less powerful position in the world. The country's trading patterns are different, while the centre of London's shipping has shifted down river to the city's new port at Tilbury, much nearer to the Thames estuary.

But, even before these changes took place, much of London's dockland area was wrecked by the bombs of World War II, and had remained a wasteland ever since.

Below: One of the best-known of London's landmarks, Tower Bridge, frames an evening view of the Thames. The roadway of the bridge, which dates from the late 19th century, is constructed as two drawbridges that can be raised to allow large ships to pass underneath.

Right: The attractions of the Thames. Boat trips from Westminster pier are as much a treat for London children as they are for visitors. In the background you can see the Charing Cross Railway Bridge spanning the river. Beyond it is the white Shell building and the Savoy Hotel.

Although the land was empty, no-one wanted it: it would have cost buyers too much to put this stricken part of London right.

By the end of the 1970s, it looked as if the last chapter had been told in the long story of London's relationship with its river – and as if the story's ending was a sad one.

London's docklands reborn

A few years later, an enormous transformation has taken place. From Tower Bridge eastwards to the Royal Docks, London's old docklands are coming to life again. Industry has been attracted by the building sites, by the light railway system that's being built, and by the promise of an airport, the 'Stolport', built on a disused wharf. Wapping, with its computerized newspaper plants, may become the Fleet Street of the 21st century. Smart private homes are being built too, and are much sought-after; in 1986, a *Sunday Times* headline called the Docklands the 'Chelsea of the east'.

Cities are no more than the surroundings that people construct for themselves. People change all the time, so cities change too. Within a handful of years, the Docklands have turned from a no hope zone into the very newest of London's 'villages'. The attractions of the Thames – with its space, its leisure opportunities, and the reflections it throws upwards on the ceilings of riverside rooms – have helped the process.

The re-birth of the Docklands is the latest, but certainly not the last, of the changes that London River has introduced to the people whose city it brought into existence.

Above: The new face of east London. Modern houses have been built in the empty spaces left by war and receding trade, and their owners have gardens in which they can sit and enjoy a breeze blowing up from the distant estuary.

Right: The Thames has always been liable to flooding, and a bad flood could put a million Londoners at risk. But, following the opening of the Thames Flood Barrier between Silvertown and Woolwich, flood danger is now a thing of the past.

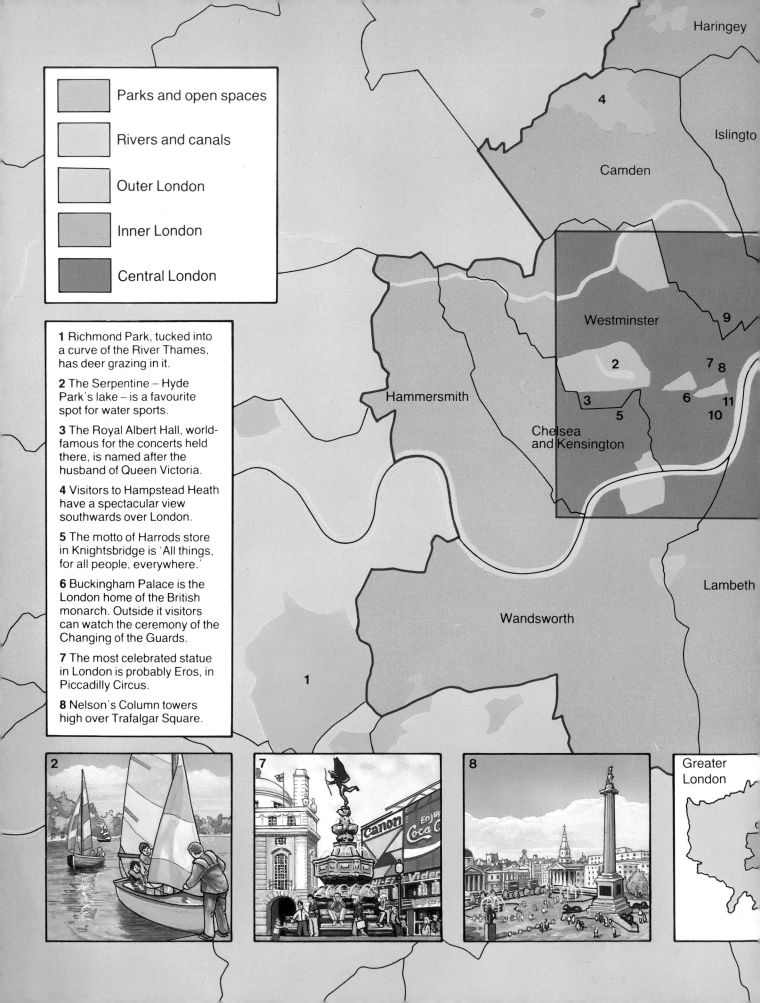

Legend

- Parks and open spaces
- Rivers and canals
- Outer London
- Inner London
- Central London

1 Richmond Park, tucked into a curve of the River Thames, has deer grazing in it.

2 The Serpentine – Hyde Park's lake – is a favourite spot for water sports.

3 The Royal Albert Hall, world-famous for the concerts held there, is named after the husband of Queen Victoria.

4 Visitors to Hampstead Heath have a spectacular view southwards over London.

5 The motto of Harrods store in Knightsbridge is 'All things, for all people, everywhere.'

6 Buckingham Palace is the London home of the British monarch. Outside it visitors can watch the ceremony of the Changing of the Guards.

7 The most celebrated statue in London is probably Eros, in Piccadilly Circus.

8 Nelson's Column towers high over Trafalgar Square.

Haringey

Islingto

Camden

Westminster

9

7 8

2

6

3   11

5   10

Hammersmith

Chelsea and Kensington

Lambeth

Wandsworth

Greater London

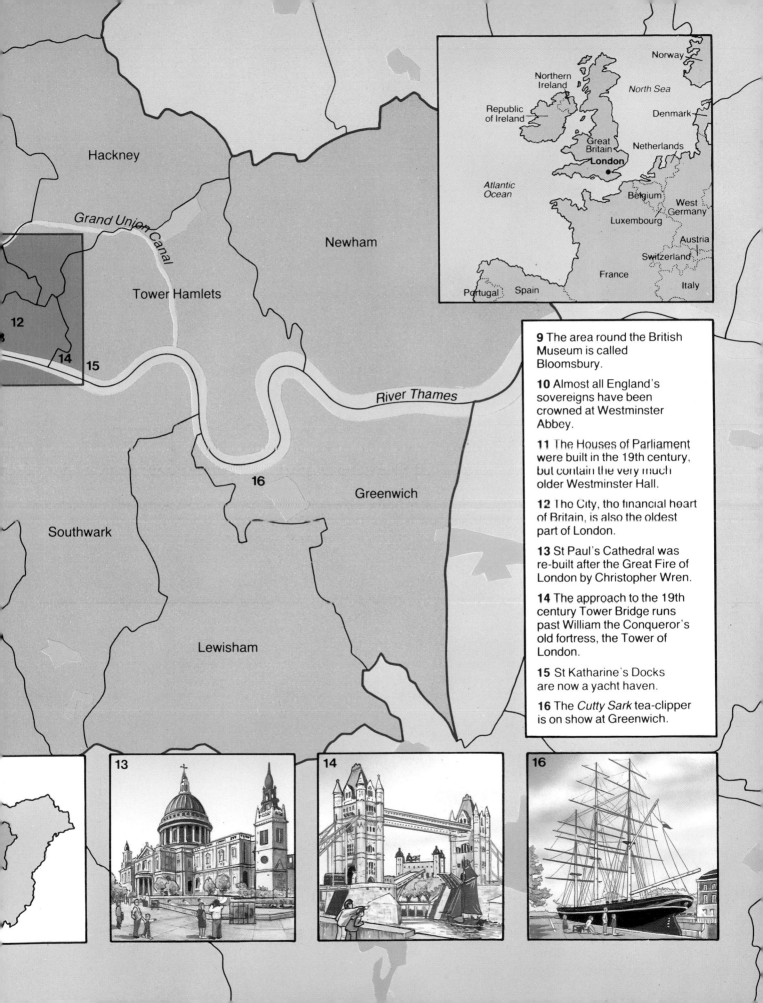

Hackney

Grand Union Canal

Tower Hamlets

Newham

12

14

15

River Thames

16

Greenwich

Southwark

Lewisham

Norway

Northern Ireland

North Sea

Republic of Ireland

Denmark

Great Britain

London

Netherlands

Atlantic Ocean

Belgium

West Germany

Luxembourg

Austria

Switzerland

France

Italy

Portugal

Spain

9 The area round the British Museum is called Bloomsbury.

10 Almost all England's sovereigns have been crowned at Westminster Abbey.

11 The Houses of Parliament were built in the 19th century, but contain the very much older Westminster Hall.

12 The City, the financial heart of Britain, is also the oldest part of London.

13 St Paul's Cathedral was re-built after the Great Fire of London by Christopher Wren.

14 The approach to the 19th century Tower Bridge runs past William the Conqueror's old fortress, the Tower of London.

15 St Katharine's Docks are now a yacht haven.

16 The *Cutty Sark* tea-clipper is on show at Greenwich.

13

14

16

Famous areas of London

London is made up of a large number of different districts all with their own distinct characters. Here are some of the better-known of them:

Bloomsbury London's 'intellectual quarter'; contains the British Museum.

Chelsea Famous for its trend-setting King's Road; the district was once cheap enough for poor artists and writers to live in, but now it's expensive.

City of London One of the great financial centres of the world. Home of the Bank of England, the Stock Exchange, Lloyd's, and of only 5 300 people. At night, it's almost empty.

Docklands Major new riverside development east of Tower Bridge.

East End The area of London east of the City: traditionally, a poor but lively district. Home of the Cockneys; but you can only be a real Cockney if you were born within the sound of the bells of St Mary-le-Bow, within the City.

Harley Street With its surrounding streets, the neighbourhood where many leading doctors and dentists have their practices.

The language of London

The main language spoken in London is English. But England is a country with many dialects, and the dialect of Old London is one of the most famous. It was spoken by the people who lived in the East End, the Cockneys, and was based on words that rhymed with each other. Instead of 'talk', you would say 'rabbit and pork'. Instead of 'hair' you would say 'Barnet Fair'. Other examples of rhyming slang are:

Noah's ark: park
Trouble & strife: wife
Mince pies: eyes
China plate: mate
Soup & gravy: navy
Plates of meat: feet
Loaf of bread: head
Sunny south: mouth

Normally, the right way to talk in rhyming slang was to use just the first word of the slang phrase: "Get off me plates", or "Get yer Barnet cut". The slang phrase for 'wife' was always the double one, though. Londoners don't speak much rhyming slang now. But some words of it are used all over the country. 'Loaf' is one, and so is 'rabbit': "How he did rabbit on" means "he just couldn't stop talking."

Knightsbridge Very elegant, very expensive. Its shops include Harrods.

Mayfair The smartest, wealthiest 'village' of them all.

Soho Just across Regent Street from Mayfair. An area that has traditionally provided a home to foreign residents in London. The south-east area of Soho, round Gerrard Street, is popular with Chinese Londoners.

Westminster With its palaces and its abbey, the heart of ruling and religious London.

West End The popular shopping area round Oxford Street and Regent Street, plus the 'theatreland' that centres on Shaftesbury Avenue and Charing Cross Road.

Books to read

There are a great many books on London: some on its history, some on its art treasures, some on its buildings and the people connected with them. Some good ones for younger readers are:
Streetwise in London by M. Perham (Mushroom Books, 1986)

The Observer's Book of London by G. Palmer and N. Lloyd (Warne, revised 1980)
London Fun Book by M. Peplow and D. Shipley (Dragon Books, 1985)
Kid's London by E. Holt and M. Perham (Pan, revised 1985)
An introduction to rhyming slang (with pictures) is given in *Rabbit & Pork: Rhyming Talk* by J. Lawrence (Cromwell (NY), 1974).

Useful addresses

You can find out more about London from the following:
British Tourist Authority, British Travel Centre, 4–12 Lower Regent Street, London SW1
London Visitor and Convention Bureau (write to their Central Information Unit, 26 Grosvenor Gardens, London SW1, or visit the Tourist Information Centre at Victoria Station).
The Museum of London, The Barbican, 150 London Wall, London EC2.

Index

Numbers in heavy type refer to picture captions, or to the pictures themselves.

PRINTED IN BELGIUM BY

INTERNATIONAL BOOK PRODUCTION

Living in
LONDON

Anna Sproule

Managing editor: Belinda Hollyer
Series editor: Polly Dunnett
Book editor: Stephen White-Thomson
Series designer: Sally Boothroyd
Book designer: Danuta Trebus
Picture researcher: Kathy Lockley
Production controller: Marguerite Fenn

Consultant: Dr J. Shepherd

The author would like to thank the staff of
the Greater London Council and of London
Regional Transport for their help during the
preparation of the text.

Cover picture: A small crowd watch the
entertainment outside the National Theatre
on the South Bank. To the north of the River
Thames, the famous dome of St Paul's
Cathedral stands out against the skyline.

Endpapers: Londoners relax in the sunshine
outside the Camden Lock market.

Title page: Londoners enjoy music from their
portable stereo system, in one of London's
many playgrounds.

Contents page: On a London housing estate,
an older man passes the time of day with a
young punk.

Page 44: Children find space to play on the
rooftops of these buildings in Islington, one
of London's boroughs.

A MACDONALD BOOK
© Macdonald & Company 1986
First published in Great Britain in 1986
by Macdonald & Company (Publishers) Ltd
London and Sydney
A BPCC plc company
All rights reserved
Made and printed by
Henri Proost, Belgium

Macdonald & Company (Publishers) Ltd
Greater London House
Hampstead Road
London NW1 7QX

Artist
Raymond Turvey 42-43

Photographic sources
Key to position of pictures:
(T) top, (C) centre, (R) right,
(L) left, (B) bottom
Ace Photo Agency: 34-35
Ardea: 39T & B
Biofotos: 38-39B
J. Allan Cash Photo Library: 13B, 19T, 34T
Daily Telegraph Colour Library: 9BR, 20BL, 22B,
    23T, 26BL & BR, 27TR, 32T
Robert Estall: 20-21B, 26B
Fotomas Index: 10-11
Sally and Richard Greenhill: title page, contents
    page, 20BR, 21TR, 23B, 27BR, 26-27T, 29TR,
    32-33B, 37T, 38TR, 40B
Robert Harding Picture Library: endpapers, 9BL,
    11T, 12C, 14B, 14-15B, 17B, 20TL & TR, 23C,
    29B, 30B, 30-31, 31T & B, 33T, 35T, 36BL, 41B
Impact Photos: 15T, 44
London Transport: 18T
Macdonald Library: 10, 11C, 12B, 36-37B
Hugh Oliff: 24, 41T
Popperfoto: 13T, 35B
Rex Features: 22-23, 29TL
Spectrum Colour Library: cover, 18B, 28
Homer Sykes: 9T, 14T, 16, 17T, 18-19B, 21TR,
    25T, 33M
ZEFA: 8, 40-41C

London boundaries:
Central London is the area within the main
British Rail stations – Paddington (west);
King's Cross, St Pancras and Euston (north);
Liverpool Street (east); and Waterloo and
London Bridge (south). Inner London is the
part built by the end of the 19th century.
Outer London is the area built in the 20th
century. The map on pages 42–43 will show
you the boundaries of Central, Inner and
Outer London.

BRITISH LIBRARY CATALOGUING IN PUBLICATION DATA

Sproule, Anna
    Living in London. – (City life)
    1. London (England) – Social life and
    customs – 20th century – Juvenile
    literature
    I. Title   II. Series
    942.1085'8   DA688

ISBN 0-356-10329-3